Contents

2 Welcome to Kew Palace

4 Family tree

6 A short history of royal Kew

11 **Palace tour:** Exterior

12 **Palace tour:** Ground floor

16 Go on, help yourself
Learn the enjoyable art of Georgian dining

20 **Palace tour:** First floor

28 An evil humour
The misdiagnosed madness of George III

32 **Palace tour:** Second floor

36 Kew Palace revealed
Peeling back the centuries-old layers

38 Lost buildings of Kew
Kew Palace is surrounded by footprints

42 The simple life
Alan Bennett recalls a visit to Kew

44 The Queen's cottage

46 A romantic box
Laurence Llewelyn-Bowen in Queen Charlotte's Cottage

48 'Bridal Nights' and 'Bum-Boats'
The royal family ridiculed

50 The inside story
Highlights of the ten-year conservation project

52 Four more palaces to explore

53 Supporting us

54 Further reading

56 Acknowledgements

Royal Kew (inside back cover)

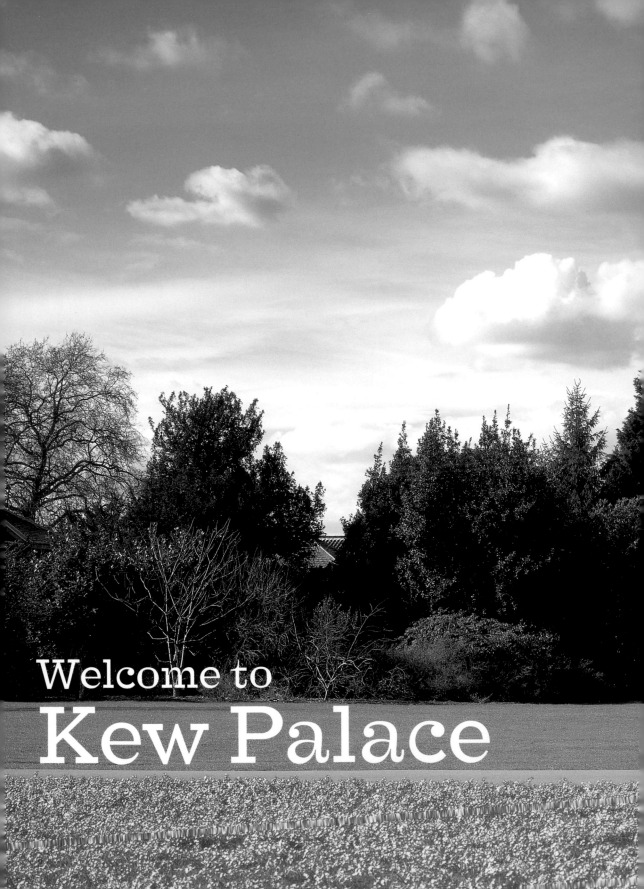

Welcome to
Kew Palace

In 1631, a City of London merchant called Samuel Fortrey built himself a fashionable, new brick mansion on the south bank of the River Thames at Kew. This became a royal home with a unique and compelling story.

Family tree

GEORGE I
(1660–1727)
= Sophia Dorothea,
Princess of Celle
(1666–1726)

GEORGE II
(1683–1760)
= Caroline,
Princess of Celle Ansbach
(1683–1737)

FREDERICK LEWIS
Prince of Wales
(1707–1751)
= Augusta,
Princess of Saxe-Gotha
(1719–1772)

Augusta
(1737–1813)
= Charles,
Duke of Brunswick
(1735–1806)

GEORGE III
(1738–1820)
= Charlotte Sophia
Princess of Mecklenburg-Strelitz
(1744–1818)

Caroline of
Brunswick
(1768–1821)
= **GEORGE IV**
(1762–1830)

WILLIAM IV
(1765–1837)
= Adelaide Princess
of Saxe-Coburg-
Meiningen
(1792–1849)

Edward
Duke of Kent
(1767–1820)
= Mary Luisa Victoria
Princess of Saxe-
Coburg-Saalfeld
(1786–1861)

Augusta
(1768–1840)

Charlotte
*(born and
died 1819)*
— Elizabeth
(1820–1821)

Frederick
Duke of York
(1763–1827)
= Frederica
Princess Royal
of Prussia
(1767–1827)

Charlotte
Princess Royal
(1766–1828)
= Frederick I
King of
Württemberg
(1754–1816)

Charlotte
(1796–1817)
= Leopold
of Saxe-
Coburg-Saalfeld
(1790–1865)

Stillborn
daughter
(1798)

QUEEN VICTORIA
(1819–1901)

George III, Queen Charlotte and their six eldest children by Johan Zoffany, 1770.

Anne, Princess Royal *(1709–1759)* = William IV, Prince of Orange *(1711–1751)*
Amelia *(1711–1786)*
Caroline *(1713–1757)*
George *(1717–1718)*
William, Duke of Cumberland *(1721–1765)*
Mary *(1723–1772)* = Frederick II, Landgrave of Hesse-Cassel *(1720–1785)*
Louisa *(1724–1751)* = Frederick V, King of Denmark *(1723–1766)*

Edward, Duke of York *(1739–1767)*
Elizabeth *(1740–1759)*
Henry, Duke of Cumberland *(1745–1790)* = Lady Anne Horton *(1742/3–1808/9)*
Louisa *(1749–1768)*
Frederick *(1750–1765)*
William, Duke of Gloucester *(1743–1805)* = Maria, Countess Dowager of Waldegrave *(1736–1807)*
Caroline *(1751–1775)* = Christian VII, King of Denmark *(1749–1808)*

Elizabeth *(1770–1840)* = Frederick Landgrave of Hesse-Homburg *(1769–1829)*

Augustus Duke of Sussex *(1773–1843)* = Cecilia Buggin Duchess of Inverness *(1785–1873)*

Mary *(1776–1857)* = William Frederick Duke of Gloucester *(1776–1834)*

Octavius *(1779–1783)*

Amelia *(1783–1810)*

Ernest Duke of Cumberland King of Hanover *(1771–1851)* = Frederica Caroline Princess of Mecklenburg-Strelitz *(1778–1841)*

Adolphus Duke of Cambridge *(1774–1850)* = Augusta of Hesse-Cassel *(1797–1889)*

Sophia *(1777–1848)*

Alfred *(1780–1782)*

George V King of Hanover *(1819–1878)*

George *(1819–1904)*

Mary Adelaide *(1833–1897)* = Francis, Duke of Teck *(1837–1900)*

Augusta *(1822–1916)* = Frederick Duke of Mecklenburg-Strelitz *(1819–1904)*

5

A short history of royal Kew

'Kew is the favourite retreat of the present King [George III] to which he goes with the Queen for a few hours every Saturday morning.'

(Diary of Count Friedrich von Kielmansegge, 1761-2)

Just as our present Queen leaves London for Windsor at the end of each week, so in the 18th century generations of royalty exchanged the intensely public life in town for more domestic retreats at Richmond and Kew.

This predictable pattern continued well into the reign of King George III (1760-1820), until 1788 when the whole nation was thrown into turmoil as the King was declared 'mad' after the onset of a mysterious illness. At this time the King still took a vital role in government, approving Parliamentary papers and appointments. Uncertainty over the state of his mental health led the Opposition – supported by the King's own son, the Prince of Wales – to call for an unheralded Regency.

However, largely due to his own strong constitution (and with little help from his doctors) the King recovered after a few months. From this time onwards his illness and brutal treatment cast a shadow over Kew and he seems never to have had such affection for it again.

Left: *The Music Party: Frederick, Prince of Wales and his Sisters* by Philip Mercier, c1733.

The history of Kew Palace has humbler origins in the first half of the previous century. In 1631 Samuel Fortrey, a Flemish merchant, built this smart, brick villa beside the Thames. It was something of a status symbol for a man of the City, whose family had escaped religious persecution in France.

For his new home he chose the site of a former courtier of Elizabeth I, perhaps that of her favourite, Robert Dudley. (The undercroft of the building survives from this time.) The house remained in Fortrey's family for another generation and then passed through a succession of wealthy tenants, including Sir Richard Levett, who became Lord Mayor of London in 1699.

Nearby Richmond had a long association with royalty since Edward III first developed his palace there. It was George II (1727-60) and his Queen, Caroline of Ansbach, with the first large royal family for many years, who were attracted to Kew Palace in 1729. They thought it very suitable as a lodging for their three eldest daughters, Anne, Caroline and Amelia.

The King and Queen continued to use Richmond Lodge (formerly in the Old Deer Park at the southern end of Kew Gardens) and the heir, Frederick, Prince of Wales rebuilt the larger White House. This stood opposite the present palace, although by all accounts there was not much love lost between the Prince (who had been brought up in Hanover) and his sisters.

Above: *Richmond Lodge* by Paul and Thomas Sandby, c1770.

So began a long connection between Kew and the Princes of Wales. Unlike his father, Frederick was very cultivated and moved easily in society. Like his mother, he employed the dazzling architect William Kent to remodel his home and then went on to lay the foundations of the botanic gardens, introducing chinoiserie garden buildings and first working with another great builder, William Chambers.

Then fate intervened when the Prince died suddenly from an infection in 1751; according to some accounts brought on by a blow from a cricket ball, a sport he enjoyed and played at Kew. His widow, Augusta, Princess of Wales, continued to develop the royal gardens. With Chambers as her architect and William Aiton, her gardener, she established the great gardens of Kew. In just six years from 1757 to 1763 Chambers added an extraordinary world in microcosm, including a mosque, a Moorish Alhambra and the great brick Pagoda.

Meanwhile, her rather shy son, George, struggled in his studies. The palace became known as the Prince of Wales's House. From 1764, George III and his young Queen took over Richmond Lodge.

Above: The Pagoda, detail from William Marlow's view of the gardens, *c*1763-5.

Right: *Augusta, Princess of Wales* by Jean-Etienne Liotard, 1754.

Left: *George III when Prince of Wales*, by Jean-Etienne Liotard, 1754 (detail).

'My hands are full of work but my pockets are not full of money. The Prince employs me three mornings a week to teach him architecture.'

(William Chambers)

Queen Charlotte with the Princess Royal by Francis Cotes, 1767; one of the King's favourite portraits.

Queen Charlotte's Cottage after G E Papendiek, *c*1820.

Children appeared with great rapidity and were lodged in various houses around Kew Green under the watchful eye of their governess, Lady Charlotte Finch. In time another Prince George – later George IV – and his brother Frederick, followed their father and were given Kew Palace until they came of age. However, in contrast, this precocious and popular George had none of his father's diligence in his studies and enthusiasm for self-improvement. He would soon embarrass his parents with his profligacy and a string of mistresses, ending with an illegal marriage to a Mrs Fitzherbert who lived at nearby Marble Hill.

In the 1770s there were plans to build a great classical palace at Richmond but these were quickly abandoned. Chambers did build the charming Observatory for the King's private astronomical observations and the Queen, in her own quiet way, added to the gardens with a *cottage orné* complete with menagerie, which the royal family enjoyed as a picnic retreat.

After his first 'King's malady', George showed less enthusiasm for improving Kew and Richmond. Then in 1800 he engaged a new architect, the capricious James Wyatt, to create a great Gothic palace, cheek by jowl with the little red brick palace. The White House, together with its miserable associations with his enforced recuperation there, was soon swept away.

The new Castellated Palace in 1819, by J Greig.

Then once more fate intervened as the King suffered two further acute outbreaks of the symptoms of porhphyria in 1801 and 1804. Each time the King was moved to Kew away from the public eye. The Castellated Palace remained an incomplete folly and was never used. Kew Palace, on the other hand, was now the only practicable home of any size left on the estate and was soon renovated in the latest fashion. Here the King would visit with his sometime estranged Queen, accompanied by their unmarried daughters who were now young women, eager to leave home.

And so their rather humdrum life at Kew remained. George III gradually declined into blindness and permanent ill health. His last visit took place in 1806 when he stopped off at the palace to dine. Then, in 1818 two momentous events occurred. The Queen was taken seriously ill en route to visit her beloved Windsor Castle and forced to stay at Kew; a day's visit extended to several months.

During this time her middle-aged sons the Dukes of Clarence and Kent were both married to German princesses in their mother's presence: the race for an heir that would eventually end with the birth of the future Queen Victoria. The Queen died at Kew on 17 November 1818, lying in state in the Dining Room before eventually being laid to rest at Windsor.

George III and Queen Charlotte walking in Kew Gardens, 1787.

From this time on the palace slept, largely ignored by the royal family. George IV considered its demolition, his brother William IV planned to double its size but these plans came to nothing. At the end of her long reign Queen Victoria, George III's granddaughter, opened the palace to the public, a relic of the royal enclave at the heart of this great centre for botanic research and conservation.

Palace tour
Exterior

Just before you enter the front door of the palace, look up and you will notice the date 1631 carved into the brickwork. This is when wealthy merchant Samuel Fortrey decided to build an impressive, double-fronted house for himself and his wife Catherine; those are her initials entwined with his in a lovers' knot.

It was a good choice of location; long before the gardens were enclosed the palace was reached by road from Kew Green, which extended right up to its front door. Visitors and tradesmen came by carriage or along the Thames flowing nearby. The palace's unknown builders interpreted the sophisticated classical style – most famously used by the Jacobean architect Inigo Jones –

entirely in a *tour de force* of rubbed and carved brick.

The exterior was modernised with sash windows in the 1730s and for many years was painted with red ochre colour wash, a practice that has recently been revived. The new lift added in 2005 takes the place of a former, clapboard privy shaft.

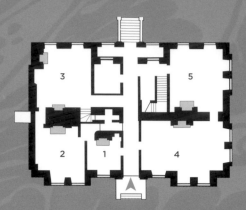

1 Ante Room
2 King's Library
3 Pages' Waiting Room
4 King's Dining Room
5 King's Breakfast Room

Palace tour
Ground floor

Throughout the palace you may encounter words narrating the story of George III and his family at Kew. These were written by playwright Jerome Vincent, based on historical letters and accounts.

Hall and Ante Room

The narrow hall connecting front and rear doors was originally open on your right, through an arched, screens passage. This would have formed a larger hall with the Dining Room. (Separate dining rooms did not become popular until the later 18th century.) You enter a small ante (or waiting) room leading to the private side of the palace. The room is characterised by its dark, linenfold panelling that dates from the early Tudor period. This is the first encounter with Kew's many recycled features, probably coming from a demolished house nearby.

Left: Today's visitor is introduced to the palace's most celebrated resident, George III, by his most lifelike image: a cast from the waxwork created from life by Madame Tussaud to celebrate the King's Golden Jubilee of 1810. Tussaud had previously had the honour of sculpting his contemporary, Louis XVI from the French King's decapitated head following the French Revolution.

King's Library

George III was passionate about books and each of his palaces had a library. His librarians bought and bound job lots of the finest books and manuscripts, some 65,000 of which later formed the nucleus of the British Library.

Princess Charlotte of Mecklenburg-Strelitz, future Queen of England, by Johann Georg Ziesenis, c1761.

This small panelled room appears to have been his library in the early 1800s. It is now a museum room, introducing the King's private world at Kew and Richmond. On the far wall is a contemporary portrait of the young Queen Charlotte by the Danish artist, Johann Georg Ziesenis, made just before her arrival in England; and a contrasting portrait bust of the King of 1813 by Peter Turnerelli.

Recent investigation of the overmantel from 1631 revealed a female classical figure from a wall painting of the mid-17th century, hidden under many layers of paint (see page 37). The room also retains its original carved decoration with 'green men' on the keystones, ancient symbols of fertility.

Today the library has a changing display of historic objects relating to George III's private life at Kew.

Pages' Waiting Room

Here the story of the palace shifts to Queen Charlotte and her large, beloved family, narrated in her voice. In her day this formed a servants' waiting room, although it has lost its partitions which divided it up into a musicians' sitting room and smaller closets.

In 1778 a member of the King's band recalled playing 'upon the lawn in Kew Garden [sic] while the King and Royal family were at dinner and in the evening...we were desired to come indoors, to try some of Handel's overtures, concertos and choruses'.

The door to your left on entering once led to the 18th-century service wing, where George III was kept secluded by his doctors in relative comfort during his illness of 1804-5. In Fortrey's time the kitchen would have occupied this entire space, centred on a much larger hearth.

King's Dining Room

This room was the scene of an extraordinary encounter in 1801, between the King and one of his medical team, Revd Thomas Willis, during his second relapse of porphyria. Willis duped his patient into meeting him here by feigning interest in the self-portrait after Van Dyck by Nogari, which once again hangs here. The King was then persuaded to leave his family and be confined in the White House opposite the palace.

This space was originally the main hall place of Fortrey's house. Remnants of its early decoration include the strapwork plaster overdoor decoration. However, the Tudor rose on the ceiling is thought to date from the time of William Kent's renovation in the mid-1730s, when the Portland stone chimney-piece was also installed.

Suppliers' accounts from the early 1800s still exist and have guided the presentation of this room. They included bills for cotton chintz curtains and somewhat unusually, a chamber organ. The original instrument has been lost and in its place is now a rare organ of the 1740s attributed to the workshop of Richard Bridge. The King loved the music of Handel, a celebrated organist as well as composer.

In the centre of the room the specially created table setting evokes encounters between George III and some of his most famous subjects and friends.

Right: *Temperance enjoying a Frugal Meal* by James Gillray, 1792. George III was renowned for his frugal eating habits: the Prime Minister once met him eating mutton chops in this room.

The doll's house in the King's Breakfast Room

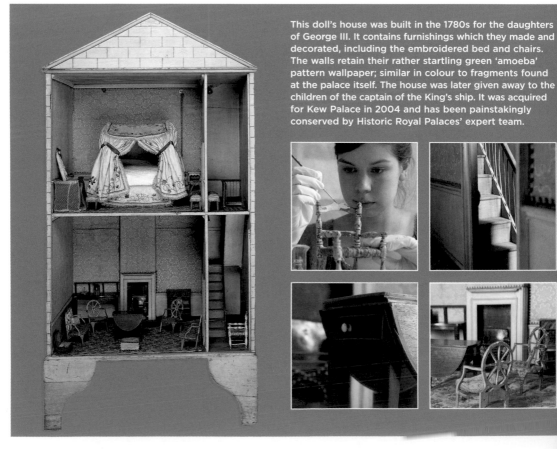

This doll's house was built in the 1780s for the daughters of George III. It contains furnishings which they made and decorated, including the embroidered bed and chairs. The walls retain their rather startling green 'amoeba' pattern wallpaper; similar in colour to fragments found at the palace itself. The house was later given away to the children of the captain of the King's ship. It was acquired for Kew Palace in 2004 and has been painstakingly conserved by Historic Royal Palaces' expert team.

King's Breakfast Room

This room takes its name from its informal function during the late Georgian period, when it contained a table with six 'Grecian shape' chairs covered in red morocco goatskin. Today it has displays and objects exploring the role Kew Palace played in the raising of three generations of royal children; in particular George III's own children. The Prince of Wales (later George IV) and his brother Frederick were allotted the palace in the 1770s until they came of age. The King expected his sons to follow the same rigid school day as he had, filled with private tutors' lessons aimed at improvement, although there was some relief such as fencing instruction in an outdoor gallery nearby.

The oak panelling of the room, with its Corinthian pilasters (possibly removed from the former hall screen), is another reminder of the house's appearance in the 1630s. This was lightened with a coat of white paint in the 1730s, which was stripped back again in the last century.

George III playing as a child by an unknown artist, c1741.

15

{SAMUEL JOHNSON, WRITER AND WIT, 1709–1784}

"HE IS *the* finest gentleman I have Ever seen."

SAMUEL JOHNSON
OF GEORGE III
1767

Go on, help yourself

Marc Meltonville, food archaeologist at Historic Royal Palaces, explains the enjoyable art of Georgian dining.

Transported back in time to the 18th century, you could sit down at any Georgian dinner table and start to feel at home.

The items placed before you on the table would, for the most part, be familiar to you.

You would recognise a knife and fork, a spoon or two, a dinner plate, napkin, bread roll, glasses and salt cellar. The Georgian world saw the start of what we think of as 'modern' dining, and many of the things we use today have their origins there.

But there are differences if we look for them: the fork with its tines, sharp and straight, the knife blade large and bulbous at the end, the wine glass with a huge foot. This equipment might be familiar, but the way in which it was all used still looked back to Tudor times.

So you would quickly have to learn to eat Georgian style.

Servants, but no service

If you were to dine at Kew Palace or any great house where rich food was served on elaborate dining wares, you would, naturally, be expected to understand the etiquette of the time.

Entering for dinner you would be most likely to see the men sitting at one end of the table and the women at the other, rather than alternating male, female as we do today. The host and hostess would take their places at the appropriate end of the table.

There might well be a house full of servants, but they would not serve you dinner. They would merely lay all the dishes for each course on the table in front of you. And what a lot of dishes! Today, when we dine out in a restaurant, the printed menu is the way of saying 'here is all the food we have, what would you like?' In a Georgian meal the host showed their wealth by having courses of food, with many dishes in each, for you to choose from, there at the table.

The more and richer the types of food in each course, the better you would think of your host. A typical first course might include a soup, listed as a 'remove' (see recipe on next page). This is because once all the guests had taken soup, served by the host, the soup tureen is 'removed' and replaced by another dish to add to the display; often a fish dish.

You, as a modern diner, might find it odd that in this first course there could well be a couple of sweet dishes to choose from. However, we still put apple sauce with pork and cranberry with turkey, so why not serve an apple pie with the meat?

The Georgian second course would resemble the first, with a good number of dishes, mostly savoury and a couple of sweet, but this time with no soup.

Your third course would be taken at a separate table, if your host had a grand enough house, and it would be covered with wonderful desserts.

In each case the guests help themselves, so you could eat as much as you like, bearing in mind our guide to good manners (see over); the servants would only help to keep the table neat and supply the drinks.

Former Prime Minister, Henry Addington dined with George III at Kew just before James Gillray published this cartoon in 1805 about his raising to the peerage. He recalled, 'I passed an hour and a half with his Majesty, and partook of his dinner, which consisted of mutton-chops and pudding.'

...nds that Fellow ...et all the Pickings.

Manners

Sit up, don't slouch.

Wash your hands before dinner.

Try not to put your elbows on the table.

Don't be too eager about the food in front of you; show restraint.

Don't make a point of mentioning the dishes you don't like.

Don't refuse a taste of anything offered to you by your host.

If you offer anyone a taste of something always give them a clean plate.

Don't dip your food in the salt; use the end of your knife to get some.

Say Grace if asked to 'do the honours'.

Adapted from *Good Manners* by Jones, 1737

To make Onion Soop

Take two Quarts of strong Veal Broth, fourteen large Onions, and cut them thin, and fry them tender; then burn half a Quarter of a Pound of Butter black; and toss up your fry'd Onions, and pit in; then stew them Half an Hour in your Broth, and take the Yolks of eight Eggs well beaten, six Spoonfuls of Spanish Wine, and put them in a quarter of an Hour before you serve up, and keep stirring it till you send it away. Let your bread be cut in Dice and fry'd.

Adapted from *Court Cookery* by R Smith, 1725

First floor

Palace tour

6   Queen's Boudoir

7   Queen's Drawing Room

8   Princess Elizabeth's Dressing Room

9   Princess Elizabeth's Bedroom

10   Queen Charlotte's Bedroom

11   Queen's Ante Room

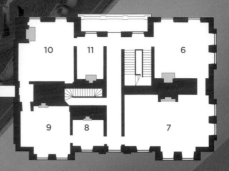

The Staircase

These stairs were constructed during William Kent's building works in the early 1730s. They are hung today with a group of paintings of Kew Gardens, made *c*1759 by J J Schalch when George III's mother, Augusta, Princess of Wales, was busy landscaping them. The replica carpet is from a runner design of the early 1800s.

Queen's Boudoir

To judge by the Charles I period plaster ceiling, with its female figures representing the Five Senses, this room has always been used for private entertaining. It is suitably intimate yet airy and well-appointed. It was in private spaces like this that the Queen and her companions would spend hours at 'women's work', as it was then known: needlework, knotting, even spinning wool like countryfolk. This is the first room on this floor where evidence of green verditer-colour wallpaper has been used to re-create the decoration of 1804-5.

The black and yellow chintz curtains are described in accounts for a small drawing room and – like the Brussels carpet – have been made from contemporary designs found in archives. Their bold colours are typical of the late-Georgian period.

The picture hang on this floor reflects the King's choice of paintings at Kew, where he amassed many works by modern Italian artists, together with older Dutch and Flemish painters that he had purchased from the Consul in Venice, Joseph Smith in 1762. Some of these can be identified by their narrow, Venetian frames with delicate floral carving. The furniture in the Boudoir reflects the taste of the Queen and princesses for the latest Greek-revival style and especially for furniture with a japanned – or painted and varnished – finish.

Plaster ceiling from the Queen's Boudoir decorated with figures representing the Five Senses.

Fragment of an early 19th-century Greek key border, found behind a shutter in the palace and re-created for the re-presentation of the building in 2005.

Queen's Drawing Room

The principal room in the house was the scene of one of the more unlikely royal events at Kew – a hastily arranged double marriage of two of the middle-aged princes, as they raced to produce an heir for the next generation. Kew was chosen because their mother, Queen Charlotte, was too ill to be moved back to London, so on 11 July 1818 William, Duke of Clarence married Princess Adelaide of Saxe-Coburg-Meiningen (meanly described as 'frightful' by one courtier) and Edward, Duke of Kent married Victoria of Saxe-Coburg-Saalfeld; a match which would produce the future Queen Victoria.

Elements of Fortrey's Great Room still dominate this interior: the large alabaster and Tournai marble chimneypiece and strapwork frieze, above plainer panelling dating from around 1700. The walls have been repainted in the pale pink of the early 19th century and on them hang some of the finest pictures in the palace, by Sebastiano and Marco Ricci and Francesco Zuccarelli.

The upholstery re-creates the original scarlet morine of the room – a popular woollen textile with watermarking. Typically for such a domestic royal home, costly silks were avoided. This was known as the Music Room in the 1800s: the harpsichord in its walnut case belonged to George III's father, Frederick, Prince of Wales, and was made by the Swiss-born Burkat Schudi.

Adelaide, Duchess of Clarence by Mary Green, *c*1820.

The Queen's Drawing Room, scene of the double royal wedding in 1818.

Princess Elizabeth's bed alcove with a reconstruction of her bed from 1805.

Princess Elizabeth's Dressing Room and Bedroom

In the Dressing Room images of satirical prints show the view of the world outside Kew on this royal family (see page 48).

When the palace was redecorated for royal occupation in 1804-5 Princess Elizabeth – the King's closest daughter – took the best apartment, moving out the King's library. The walls were lined to create arched recesses in the manner of architect John Soane and hung with the green verditer wallpaper, traces of which can still be seen. Here Elizabeth had a Grecian couch-bed furnished with 'one stripe' yellow and red chintz. This has been re-created based on contemporary designs. The curtains are draped over Cupid's bows, an optimistic motif for a princess who was desperate to be married. Behind all this on one wall the older house is revealed, showing a former servant's doorway in one corner. The coarse plaster is made with animal hair.

Princess Elizabeth seated with her two elder sisters by Thomas Gainsborough, 1793-4. She effectively ran the household during the King's recurring illness.

'...the old housekeeper shewed us the room in which she died – her Chair tied across with a piece of tape that no one might rest on it since she left it – her room exactly in the same order as when she left it, all this resulting from the affectionate reverence with which these poor attendants regarded her'.

Queen Charlotte's Bedroom

...this was the scene shortly after Queen Charlotte's merciful death at Kew on 17 November 1818, following a prolonged stay here *en route* to Windsor. She had been devotedly attended by Princess Augusta above all her children. Surprisingly, the Queen used this small, unmodernised room and appears not to have followed her daughters' fashions. She had a liking for dimity – a plain-coloured, cotton cloth, used in the bed re-created here in the style of Thomas Sheraton. She preferred religious pictures or family portraits in her rooms, a reflection of two of her principal interests.

Queen Charlotte in 1814, after Henry Edridge.

Queen's Ante Room

The Queen's Ante Room has been left stripped of its 20th-century wallpaper to reveal more of the older history of the building. Beneath the surface you can see the fingerprints of 18th-century plasterers and crude marbling above the fireplace from a century earlier. A section of the re-created green verditer wallpaper has been hung to show the hand-processes involved.

The story of the King's life closes here with a display about his final days.

George III during his last Illness
Attributed to Joseph Lee *c*1820.

Left: Queen Charlotte's Bedroom with the horsehair chair in which she died.

An evil humour

George III by Johan Zoffany, 1771 (detail).

The 'madness' of King George III is now thought to be the hereditary blood disorder known as porphyria. His perplexed doctors administered what seems to us a barbaric treatment regime; today symptoms can be controlled by drugs. Professor Martin Warren explains this distressing illness.

WHEN King George III complained in 1788 that his 'water had turned red' his doctors were troubled; no one had any intimation that his condition would deteriorate to the extent that eventually he would be unfit to rule. This was the first of three major attacks which severely affected him, both mentally and physically. He was confined at Kew where, out of the public gaze, an increasingly desperate band of doctors tried to cure him.

In the 18th century, porphyria was unknown as a disease. Today it remains difficult to diagnose, but if it is there is a much greater understanding of what is wrong with the patient. We now know that porphyria (from the Greek word for red/purple) is a complex metabolic disorder associated with the formation of haem, the red pigment that gives blood its colour.

Little wonder the King hated the medical profession.

George III developed a mixture of symptoms which confused his doctors, who could describe his illness only as an 'evil humour' that progressed from his legs to his brain. The King displayed a number of neurological symptoms, including muscle weakness, abdominal pain, constipation, insomnia and agitation. His psychiatric manifestations – among them constant talking and violent outbursts – were misdiagnosed as madness.

Competing doctors sought to treat the King's constipation by the administration of purgatives and emetics. These did no good and probably worsened his condition. They also tried hot and cold baths and leeching. With the onset of his mental derangement, the services of Dr Willis, a keeper of a provincial madhouse, were sought on the advice of the wife of one of the King's equerries, whose mother had been treated by the physician.

Reverend Doctor Francis Willis by John Russell, 1789.

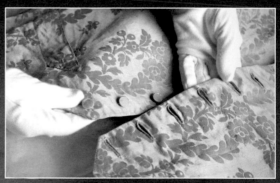
Detail of the King's silk waistcoat, worn in his final days and specially adapted for the ailing monarch.

Willis employed a regime of intimidation, coercion and restraint; the King was put into a strait-jacket (which he referred to as his hated 'waistcoat') if he refused to do as he was asked. Little wonder that the King hated the medical profession.

George recovered from his first major attack in March 1789 (more despite his treatment than because of it) and there was much rejoicing. Grand balls were held to celebrate his return to health, and many commemorative items were made for royal supporters. However, he suffered recurrences in 1801 and 1804 and then went into a severe decline in 1810. A Regency was declared in 1811.

George III died at Windsor Castle on 19 January 1820, senile, blind and deaf, unaware that his beloved wife Charlotte had died two years previously.

What causes porphyria?

The haem molecule in the blood is made from the action of a number of enzymes. If any of these enzymes become impaired, as the result of a genetic mutation or by some external chemical or drug, then there is a chance that the patient will suffer with porphyria.

There are various types, with symptoms ranging in severity. However, porphyria is extremely rare, affecting 1 in 5000 people worldwide. The disease is hereditary, but the faulty gene can skip several generations. Genetic testing is now available to identify families at risk, but fortunately, most who have a faulty gene do not develop any symptoms of the disease.

What are the symptoms?

The symptoms of porphyria are many and varied, which makes the disorder so difficult to diagnose. Some types of porphyria can cause a range of changes, from sleeplessness and agitation to severe abdominal pain and muscle weakness. In more serious attacks the patient can suffer with temporary mental derangement.

Other types of porphyria result largely in skin blemishes, where certain chemicals in the blood react with sunlight to produce blistering, making the patient very photosensitive.

There are also a few examples of porphyria that result in the patient suffering with both neurological and skin symptoms. It is one of these mixed types that is thought to have affected George III.

For further information about porphyria, visit the Porphyria Society at **www.porphyria.org.uk**

orphyria, /po'firia/noun, 18thc. Equiv./

n inherited metabolic disorder causing
bdominal pain, skin lesions and
sychiatric disturbances

eorge III suffered from an acute and
ntermittent form of this cruel illness,
vhich his doctors misdiagnosed as
nadness

Palace tour

Second floor

12 Closets
13 Princess Augusta's Bedroom
14 Princess Amelia's Bedroom
15 Princess Amelia's Dressing Room

The bedroom floor has largely been abandoned since 1818.

Its rooms evoke the sometimes lonely world of the princesses who stayed here. They are a remarkable survival for a royal home, especially in London where fashion dictated frequent redecoration. Although well-worn, this floor provides a rich source of information about how the palace was built in the 1630s and changed over its first two centuries: all this has been used during its most recent restoration.

A feature common throughout is the re-use of older panelling of all different periods, as larger rooms were subdivided over the years. In the corridor are newly commissioned photographs giving a glimpse of the shadowy world of the servants' attics upstairs – a warren of irregularly-shaped rooms barely penetrated by daylight. Unfortunately, the rooms are too fragile to open to visitors, but you can read more about them on page 36.

Princess Augusta by
Sir William Beechey, *c*1800 (detail).

Princess Augusta's Apartment

An uncommon arrangement of small rooms, comprising an outer and inner 'light closet' (with its own sash window) leads to Princess Augusta's Bedroom. This would have been used by a personal attendant. You can still see traces of mid-Georgian floral wallpaper surviving and the joinery still has its pink lead paint, similar to that re-created in the hall. Princess Augusta was the eldest sister to live at the palace in the early 1800s, when she was in her thirties. The diarist and author Fanny Burney called her 'exquisite' and some thought her the most attractive of the princesses, yet she failed to find a longed-for husband. The older children's own words here conjure up their confined existence at Kew, where they relied on letters as a window on the wider world.

the most attractive...

Princess Amelia's Apartment

The neighbouring apartment belonged to the youngest princess, Amelia, who was the King's favourite. She died suddenly of tuberculosis in 1810, an event which pushed her father into his final decline and prompted the Regency. This room is full of reminders of her brief time here: her bed alcove where she too had a Grecian couch-bed like her sister Elizabeth, a genuine Gothic fireplace specially put in for her and many traces of decoration. Her rooms though small were comfortable, with a dressing room and even her own water closet. A late Georgian flushing toilet – the latest technology in its day – has been put back here.

Visitors return to the hall by the main staircase.

Princess Amelia by Andrew Robertson, 1810.

the favourite.

Kew Palace revealed

The extensive renovation of Kew Palace has given historians and archaeologists a wonderful opportunity.

Curator Lee Prosser exposes some of the secrets that have been uncovered.

The early history of Kew Palace lies in shadows.

Externally, the rubbed and shaped bricks on the façade evoke the early 17th-century building, but how the interior appeared in its first life as a merchant's house around the time of the English Civil War is very poorly known. Many secrets lie hidden beneath layers of paint and in inaccessible nooks and crannies, and archaeology has been used to make the most of these fragments.

The long period when the palace was closed in the 1990s presented a golden opportunity to explore areas of the building which are never normally visible: beneath the floorboards, in the attics and behind panelling.

Paint analysis illustrates the long sequence of redecoration in a building. By removing small pieces of the paint and magnifying the sample, a cross-section can reveal centuries of build-up as rooms were repainted frequently.

In the King's Library, 22 layers of paint were identified on the early 17th-century panelling, revealing a range of stone colours, off-whites and occasionally darker, more adventurous tones applied as fashions changed and painted walls became grubby with open fires burning in the room. This kind of detailed study has revealed the whole world of Kew to the light of modern knowledge.

A fragment of a female form has been uncovered.

In the King's Library, a niche to the side of the fireplace was modified in the 1960s with shelves. When these were removed, the 17th-century painted panelling was revealed, showing that the room once had a rich, dark effect with swirls of yellow ochre and scallop shells painted on to brown panelling.

An expensive figurative scheme painted entirely in shades of white and grey, of which a fragment of a female form has been uncovered, was also painted during this time. All over the house, paint and scraps of wallpaper have revealed the wider story, and the sequence by which the building was altered and modified in the 18th and 19th centuries.

Left: 17th-century wall painting, discovered in the King's Library.

Carved into the oak beams are 'witch' or protection marks.

The higher you climb, the less the house has changed, and the roof of the palace preserves some of the most extraordinary traces of past times. The rooms where the daughters of George III lived have changed little since 1816, when their illustrious occupants last stayed there.

We don't know much about the servants and lesser members of the household who lived in the attics and kept the palace running, but Samuel Fortrey's original roof survives, and carved into several of the oak beams are ritual protection marks, sometimes known as 'witch' marks.

These curious symbols were placed near vulnerable openings such as windows and fireplaces by the superstitious inhabitants of these spaces, who believed that evil spirits could enter the house, bewitch the hapless sleeping occupants or even substitute babies with 'changelings'.

Such was the strength of belief among country people in the early 17th century that everything from doors to chimneypieces might be marked to ward off evil. The symbols often take the form of the letter M, invoking the Blessed Virgin Mary, or interlocking circles. So often overlooked as 'doodles' or carpentry marks, they like many other aspects are part and parcel of the rich archaeological heritage the building has to offer.

'Witch' mark on a roof beam, from the early years of the palace.

The royal family once strolled around a fantasy world at Kew, created for them by William Chambers. As Curator Sebastian Edwards explains, only a handful of these exotic buildings survive, but much of his vision remains on paper.

Under the sweeping lawns and glorious flowerbeds of Kew lie traces of an extraordinary collection of buildings, created by some of the most exciting architects of the day for their enlightened royal patrons.

In 1763, the ambitious Williams Chambers, favourite royal architect, looked back over more than a decade of building and decided to pay for the publication of a lavish book to publicise his work at Kew: an exotic landscape, inspired by the gardens of ancient Rome, China and other foreign shores. By strolling a mere one and a half miles, the royal family could enjoy a fantasy world tour taking in 20 buildings as they journeyed across continents and time. Other architects both before and after Chambers brought this number closer to 60.

Lost buildings of Kew

Today, only an odd handful has survived the vagaries of royal taste aided by the hand of fate. The iconic Pagoda still stands, with Chambers's Orangery, the ruined arch folly and the rebuilt Temple of Aeolus – open to the god of winds. The King's Observatory is now stranded in the middle of a modern golf course and the practical Ice House still remains, protected from the elements underground.

Visiting Kew Gardens now, it is hard to visualise how different the landscape must have been, and to realise how much of Chambers's and other architects' work has been erased from the map.

William Chambers's protégé, the architect John Soane, used his 'infinity of buildings...of the taste and manners of the different nations' at Kew to inspire his students at the Royal Academy. This illustration, taken from his lecture notes of c1820, places the Temple of the Sun at the centre, radiating the light of ancient classical architecture across the globe. However, the Kew Palace of today is not included – dismissed as a 'nursery or a residence for superior domestics' in 1819. In its place Soane's draughtsman drew instead William Kent's White House, which in George III's time was known as Kew Palace.

Soane's tribute to his master also left out several more extraordinary lost buildings not associated with Chambers. William Kent had created two rather strange grottos for Queen Caroline in the 1730s, one of which survived well into the 19th century. And then there was George III's grandiose folly, the Castellated Palace. This huge, 'cardboard gothick' building was designed by the capricious James Wyatt to be another Windsor, but closer to London and so more convenient than the real thing.

Building began in 1801; however, the King's recurring ill health and spiralling costs (which reached half a million pounds) soon led to its abandonment. Determined to remove this embarrassing reminder of his father's excesses, George IV had to resort to explosives to demolish the building a few years later as it was built partly from cast iron.

The White House, known in George III's day as Kew Palace. William Kent rebuilt an old Tudor mansion in the latest Palladian style for Frederick, Prince of Wales from 1731. It had splendid Roman-inspired interiors and a double-height hall. When George III and his family moved in in 1772 Chambers improved upon it more, but it was demolished only 30 years later, a memorial to the King's illness there.

Gothic Cathedral. This rather sophisticated design was by Horace Walpole's architect at Strawberry Hill, J H Müntz, and built within sight of the Pagoda. Like many of Kew's buildings it was constructed of wood and painted to look like stone. But also, like so many 'Gothick' buildings of its time it only lasted a few decades.

The Palladian Bridge by Chambers, 1757. Inspired by the designs of 16th-century Italian architect

Andrea Palladio, this elegant timber bridge was put up in one night, to the delight of the Dowager Princess of Wales. It appears in two paintings in the palace by J J Schalch.

The Mosque, 1761. Chambers claimed to be 'adhering to ...Turkish architecture' but the inside of his mosque was decidedly Western, with stucco palm trees and its ceiling painted with a sunny sky by the artist Richard Wilson. It lasted a mere 18 years.

The House of Confucius. This very early orientalist building was constructed by the lake for Frederick, Prince of Wales by the painter Joseph Goupy in 1749. Its interior was filled with scenes of the lives of Confucius, all sadly lost. The young Chambers may also have had a hand in its design and he later moved it to the head of the lake.

Above left: *Lecture diagram of all the buildings in Kew Gardens*, Office of Sir John Soane, c1820.

The simple life

Playwright and author Alan Bennett, who wrote the play, and the subsequent screenplay for the film, The Madness of King George, recalls his visit to 'modest' Kew.

I have only once been to Kew, a shocking admission when I have lived half my life in London, and saying Kew I mean both the palace and the gardens, both to me largely unknown.

The occasion of my solitary visit was in 1994 when we were about to embark on the filming of *The Madness of King George*, which tells the story of the King's first period of mental instability which occurred in 1788. Originally confined at Windsor, the King was later moved to Kew where it was thought he would be less in the public eye. Kew was also a more convenient location for his doctors, it being as true then as now, however critical an illness, it must always yield to the convenience of the therapist.

When Nicholas Hytner and I came to look at Kew Palace in 1994 it wasn't entirely clear in my mind that this was the building that had housed George III in 1788-9. It was there, of course, but the King and his entourage were mainly housed in the White House, a long, low 18th-century building that stood nearby and which was demolished soon after. It was only the later bouts of 'madness' that saw George III confined in Kew Palace itself. I remember on our visit being shown the high banisters on the stairs, which were tall enough to stop the royal patient throwing himself over. That apart though, there was no evidence of his unhappy tenancy.

As a building the palace itself is quite modest and hardly lives up to the notion of a palace at all. This is because it started off as the house of a 17th-century merchant of Flemish descent, hence its style. But the style, too, is deceptive and more familiar in Holland than in England where most buildings of this type date from the late 19th century when it was popular in revival. Delightful though it is, Kew Palace nevertheless suggests something in the region of Cadogan Square.

The modesty of the house and its rural situation were what recommended it to George III and his Queen, who like other 18th-century monarchs, liked to play at being simple people who found the unpretentiousness of Kew an ideal setting.

With George III though, it wasn't simply a case of Happy Families. He was a good family man and punctilious though he was in matters of royal etiquette, in other ways he was straightforward and down to earth. With the exception of his eldest son (always a Hanoverian blind spot) he was a devoted father, a faithful husband and happiest with his family around him. His interest in agriculture was not feigned and, shy though he was, he was on easy terms with the shopkeepers of Windsor besides being up in all the latest scientific and industrial advances. He has a claim to being the most cultivated monarch ever to have graced the throne.

Having been so happy at Kew it is ironic that when he was brought there wild and distracted in November 1788 it was under duress and false pretences. In order to induce him to co-operate and go to Kew he was promised that there he would be united with Queen Charlotte from whom he had been forcibly separated at Windsor. This proved to be a lie. He was housed in one set of rooms with the Queen upstairs and it was only when his health began to improve that they were allowed to spend time together.

The King had also been reluctant to go to Kew because quite sensibly he knew it was a summer house and not equipped for winter occupation. In the film *The Madness of King George* Kew was impersonated by Thame Park in Oxfordshire. Artificial snow was laid across the lawns and though we were filming in almost tropical temperatures it was still possible to look at the setting and shiver.

The White House, which in some ways Thame Park did resemble, has gone now, demolished in 1802 and the Castellated Palace that was meant to replace it was planned but never completed. Instead there is the palace itself and even though the King was to be confined here in later years when he was 'mad' it still seems a happy house, not quite a doll's house but a palace by default.

Paradoxically, it's Windsor with its glazed brick and elaborate crenellations that looks like a 19th-century mental institution, with Kew the ideal home.

The Queen's cottage

Queen Charlotte's Cottage was a rustic retreat from the cares of the world for the royal family. Curator Sebastian Edwards traces its elusive history.

Queen Charlotte could hardly have been accused of inciting revolutionary feeling but around 1771, in Richmond Gardens, she created an early example of a *cottage orné,* a rustic retreat. This was an act which a few years later contributed to the demise of her French counterpart, Marie Antoinette, when she built her model hamlet at Versailles to affect the life of a peasant. They were soon to rise up and chop off her head.

No doubt the Queen was inspired by her gardener at Richmond, 'Capability' Brown, who was so influential in introducing the picturesque movement to the landscapes of English aristocrats.

Perhaps uniquely, the cottage reflects her personal taste and interests. Here she could follow new ideas in the more natural style of gardening, just as her predecessor Queen Caroline (consort of George II) had done here two generations before, when she employed the gardener Charles Bridgeman alongside William Kent.

It was a perfect location for a modest retreat where the Queen and the rest of the royal family could enjoy private picnics or take tea during long summer walks through the gardens. However, there were plenty of servants for the kitchen from Richmond Lodge nearby.

The cottage overlooked a new menagerie, which must have delighted the growing numbers of royal children. It was first home to pheasants and other exotic birds, but by 1792 also contained some of the first kangaroos to arrive in Britain.

The Print Room

Although the exterior of the cottage is carefully contrived to look extremely rustic, its strict symmetry and sophisticated interior suggest that an architect must have helped Queen Charlotte balance any rural fantasy with elegance and comfort. It may have been William Chambers, given his popularity at Kew and his occasional forays into 'primitive' architecture.

Beneath the cottage's thatched roof the half-timbered walls are rather crude, and show marks of pre-fabrication. These may have been partly rendered at first. Inside, the building consists of a hall on either side, with family to the left, servants to the right, each with very similar, sweeping staircases. In the centre there is a small salon, called the Print Room and above, the Picnic Room.

The **Print Room** is hung with over 150 satirical engravings, mostly after William Hogarth. These were 'of elegance and humour' according to *The London Magazine* of 1774, although the writer could not believe that certain political scenes were a suitable choice for a queen. The terracotta-tiled floor completes the rustic appearance of this room.

Upstairs, the **Picnic Room** is more unusual: it has two full-height windows (taken from a 17th-century building) that would have provided an advantageous view of the menagerie and the wilderness. The paintings of trailing nasturtiums and convolvulus, evoking a bower, are believed to be the work of Princess Elizabeth, the most artistic of the daughters of George III. They may have

been part of her preparations for the King's intended visit in 1805 – one of his last to Kew. Alas, the occasion was rained off.

On the ground floor, seen through the glazed door, is a small kitchen where cooks could prepare the impromptu picnics.

The cottage was looked back on as 'a favourite place with the King', but its heyday was brief, and George III did not return to Kew after 1806. It was used for the last time by the royal family in 1818 following the double wedding of the Duke of Clarence (later William IV) and Edward, Duke of Kent (father of Queen Victoria).

Queen Victoria rarely visited the cottage, although it was maintained by a housekeeper throughout her reign. In 1898 the Queen gave the cottage and its grounds to the public to commemorate her Diamond Jubilee.

The cottage is furnished with a changing display of period furniture and equipment from the Royal Collection, the Victoria & Albert Museum and the Science Museum, London.

Queen Charlotte's Cottage was a revelation to me. I'd always rather fondly imagined life for the family of George III as a cosy gentlemanly affair, not pompous grandiloquent or fussily royal like the court of Louis XVI in France at the same time. And in Queen Charlotte's Cottage I can really see an environment that was specifically created for intimate personal experiences that I'm sure stayed with the family as fond memories throughout their lives.

Since the British are such very passionate gardeners, I've always thought that the buildings they erect in their gardens are so much more 'them' than the mansions they might build for themselves to live in. Garden buildings like Queen Charlotte's Cottage seem so much more lyrical, more whimsical, and so far away from the architectural bombast of the 'dress to impress school of building' that set the tone for the main house.

The understated crinkle-crankle exterior of the cottage (rather like the cottage of Sleeping Beauty's fairy godmother) gives no clue to the ornamental symmetry and practical classicism of what's inside. I love that, a romantic box for a pragmatic family to picnic in. And inside it's the first floor salon with its deep windows and gorgeous views that takes the breath away. It's like a tree house, an effect the painted decoration works hard to get across.

It is thought Princess Elizabeth, one of George III's younger daughters painted the *trompe l'oeil* pergola of bamboo draped in nasturtiums and convolvulus. She was a very talented artist, who trained under the flower painters, Margaret Meen and Mary Moser.

It does make sense that she would wish to embellish such a personal place with her own very personal take on decorating. And it's not hard to imagine a tea party to celebrate the unveiling of her decorations with the noises of her assembled family coming up the stairs as she, a little nervous, opens the door with a flourish to show them exactly what she's been up to.

I first saw it on a cold winter morning, grey and overcast, there was either a cold rain or wet snow in the air. I was overwhelmed by first how summery the room felt, even though the view through the windows was quite obviously the opposite. And I suppose that's exactly what the room was conceived to do. To create a light-filled tree house, a mid-summer bonnet, the perfect fantastical background to happy family memories.'

Interior designer Laurence Llewelyn-Bowen gives a first impression of Queen Charlotte's Cottage.

A romantic

'...a light-filled tree house, a mid-summer bonnet, the perfect fantastical background to happy family memories'.

box

'Bridal Nights' and 'Bum-Boats'

Some of these 18th-century satirical prints are enough to make even the most fervent anti-monarchists blush warns Curator Caroline Cliffe.

Virtually every major event of George III's reign can be traced through satirical prints – the political 'cartoons' of the day. By the end of the 18th century, London was awash; prints appearing in pamphlets, on the walls of coffee houses and in specialist print shops where the latest editions displayed in the windows attracted large crowds. These prints were the 'popular press' of the day, and arguably more shocking and funny than the most lurid and outrageous of our tabloid tales today. Then, as now, it was crucial for caricaturists to respond quickly to events before they became 'yesterday's news'. Visually striking, they could be enjoyed by everyone – the Prince of Wales, one of those most savagely satirised, was an enthusiastic patron.

1

2

3

1. *The Bridal Nights* James Gillray 1797

Bearing candles and a bowl of posset, the King and Queen lead their eldest daughter, aged 31, to her bridal bed. The bridegroom, the Prince of Württemberg, is so fat that his brother-in-law, the Prince of Wales, merely looks a little stout by comparison!

2. *Taking Physick; – or – The news of Shooting the King of Sweden!* James Gillray 1792

As revolution swept Europe, monarchies came under threat. Gillray leaves the King and Queen no dignity as he shows them seated on thrones of a rather different kind! They hear with horror from Prime Minister Pitt that the King of Sweden has been shot.

3. *The Introduction* James Gillray 1791

When George III's second son, Frederick, Duke of York, married a Prussian princess it was mistakenly believed that she came with an enormous dowry. With a reputation for miserliness, the King and Queen's excitement is unbridled as they meet the bride!

The most famous satirical caricaturist of the 18th century is James Gillray (1756-1815). When he met George III all the artist received from his monarch was 'a look' – a glance at this page and one can only imagine what that look would have conveyed!

4

5

6

4. *The French Invasion; – or – John Bull, bombarding the Bum-Boats* James Gillray 1793

Yes, he's doing exactly what you think he's doing! Giving a whole new meaning to the 'body politic', the King literally embodying his country (John Bull), defecates on the invading French bum-boats (service boats).

5. *Affability* James Gillray 1795

With his own three farms at Windsor, the King had the disconcerting habit of visiting his rural subjects unannounced. This terrified yokel shrinks from 'Farmer George' who bombards him with questions. The Queen, dumpy in headscarf and smock, hangs on the King's arm, clutching a box of her beloved snuff.

6. *A Voluptuary under the horrors of Digestion* James Gillray 1792

The future Regent's gross appetite and debauched lifestyle gave satirists plenty of inspiration. His stomach bursting from his breeches, the Prince of Wales slumps in a chair picking his teeth with a fork; he is surrounded by evidence of his excesses, most revoltingly an overflowing chamber pot.

Visitors to Kew may find it hard to imagine that this lovely little palace, resplendent in its distinctive red limewash, with an interior full of surprises, was so recently in danger of being closed indefinitely.

The fight to conserve this remarkable building began in 1996, when a survey of the leaks in the roof revealed the deteriorating condition of the whole building. It was clearly time for major building repairs.

The palace was closed to the public and the contents removed and returned to lenders. Our aim was to undertake a major envelope repair to make the building weather-tight, while planning internal repairs and interpretation. Curators devoted hundreds of hours to meticulous research which informed the interpretation proposals, while discoveries made during the repair project convinced us still further of the incredible potential of the building.

The discovery of a patch of red pigment behind a dilapidated hopper at the top of a drainpipe indicated that the whole exterior of the palace had been colour-washed. We decided to reapply the pigment, a controversial decision for a Scheduled Ancient Monument. However, our application was approved in 1998.

Painting the exterior of the palace with red limewash.

Lead Surveyor and Project Sponsor Jo Thwaites describes some of the highlights of the project to conserve Kew Palace.

The inside story

Right: Plain doors were given an oak-grained effect using traditional materials and techniques.

Far right: Conserving the 17th-century plaster decoration on the ceiling of the Queen's Boudoir.

The scale of the internal repairs uncovered areas of the building that had remained unseen for over 270 years: 17th-century wall paintings, fragments of wallpaper and hidden nooks and crannies all emerged into the light.

It was decided to present some rooms as they would have been enjoyed by George III and his family in the early years of the 19th century, using authentic colour schemes and materials. Rich draperies, carpets and furnishings were specially commissioned, from descriptions in original bills of sale and 19th-century designs.

Specialists were brought in to paint and wallpaper and to study the historic timbers, fixtures and fittings. The latest techniques of paint analysis have informed all the colours used on the walls and joinery in the palace.

Traces of 18th and early 19th-century wallpaper were found by an expert, who analysed the fragments and re-created the paper in its original sheet sizes, and the green verditer colour, grinding pigments until a match was found. She and her team also hand-made the Greek key flock border (above), based on a date-stamped fragment found behind a shutter in the palace.

We also chose to leave some of the upper rooms – untouched for over 200 years – just as they were when they were abandoned by George III's daughters, revealing the structure of the house. The original lath and plaster is clearly visible in several areas; in places you can still see the workmen's thumbprints.

Research suggested that we could use existing openings to an 18th-century water closet shaft on the west side of the palace to install a lift, which now allows level access to every floor. At every stage of the project we were helped by a group of local people, with a range of abilities and disabilities, who advised on both physical and intellectual access.

Each century has left its mark on the palace, and a great joy of working at Kew has been uncovering these, and ensuring they remain for future generations to study and appreciate.

It was with a great sense of pride – and relief – after ten event-filled years that we witnessed the official opening of the palace on 5 May 2006 by HRH The Prince of Wales.

This has been the project of a lifetime, and it's been an honour to be part of it all.

Four more palaces to explore;
hundreds of stories to discover

Tower of London

Gaze up at the massive White Tower, tiptoe through a king's medieval bedchamber and marvel at the Crown Jewels. Meet the Yeoman Warders with bloody tales to tell; stand where famous heads rolled and prisoners wept...then discover even more surprising stories about the Tower!

Recorded information: 0870 756 6060

Banqueting House

Walk in the footsteps of a dazzling company of courtiers who once danced, drank and partied beneath the magnificent Rubens's painted ceiling. This revolutionary building was created for court entertainments, but is probably most famous for the execution of Charles I in 1649. Spare him a thought as you gaze up at this ravishing painting – one of his last sights on earth...

Recorded information: 0870 751 5187

Hampton Court Palace

Explore Henry VIII's magnificent palace, then stroll through the elegant Baroque apartments and glorious formal gardens of William III and Mary II. Feel the heat of the vast Tudor Kitchens and the eerie chill of the Haunted Gallery, before you disappear into the fiendish Maze...

Recorded information: 0870 752 7777

Kensington Palace

Marvel at the stunning collection of English court dress at this stylish palace, a unique archive of royal fashion from the 18th century to the present day – including several evening dresses worn by Diana, Princess of Wales. Explore the magnificent State Apartments and take tea in the Orangery designed for Queen Anne in 1704.

Recorded information: 0870 751 5170

We offer an exciting program of events and exhibitions throughout the year. For more information and details on tickets and how to find us, please visit **www.hrp.org.uk**

Supporting us

Historic Royal Palaces is the independent charity that looks after the Tower of London, Hampton Court Palace, the Banqueting House, Kensington Palace and Kew Palace. We help everyone explore the story of how monarchs and people have shaped society in some of the greatest palaces ever built.

We receive no funding from the Government or the Crown so we depend on the support of our visitors, members, donors, volunteers and sponsors.

Can you help?

We hope that you have thoroughly enjoyed your visit to Kew Palace and have discovered more about the conservation of this precious building. Our work goes on; funds will always be needed to protect and maintain the palace. Any donation that you can spare means this valuable work can continue. Please call the Development Department on **0845 389 3003** for more information, or email **development@hrp.org.uk**. Thank you.

Join us!

Joining Historic Royal Palaces is the perfect way to explore the inside stories of five extraordinary places that helped define our nation's history. What's more, you'll save money and contribute to the important work of conserving the palaces at the same time.

It's amazing value; membership of Historic Royal Palaces means you have the freedom to visit Hampton Court Palace, the Tower of London, Kensington Palace, the Banqueting House and Kew Palace (open April – September) as often as you like. Membership also means you don't have to queue – simply walk in to see, experience and understand what made us who we are. Other benefits include exclusive members-only events, behind-the-scenes tours and great discounts in our shops and online.

Make a present of the past

Step through the doors of a royal palace and you are surrounded by stories of strategy, intrigue, ambition, romance, devotion and disaster. What more inspiring gift could there be than a Historic Royal Palaces Membership for someone who shares your love of history, amazing buildings, their beautiful contents and gorgeous gardens?

To enquire about becoming a member of Historic Royal Palaces and for more information on the range of benefits you receive please visit **www.hrp.org.uk** or call **0870 751 5174**.

Further reading

Blomfield, D. *Kew Past*, Phillimore, 1994

Cloake, J. *Palaces and Parks of Richmond and Kew*, (2 vols), Phillimore, 1995-6

Desmond, R. *Kew: The History of the Royal Botanic Gardens*, The Harvill Press, 1995

Fraser, F. *The Six Daughters of George III*, John Murray, 2005

Groom, S and Prosser, L. *Kew Palace: The Official Illustrated History*, Merrell Publishers, 2006

Hibbert, C. *George III*, Viking, 1998

Roberts, J (ed). *George III and Queen Charlotte: Patronage, Collecting and Court Taste*, Royal Collection, 2004

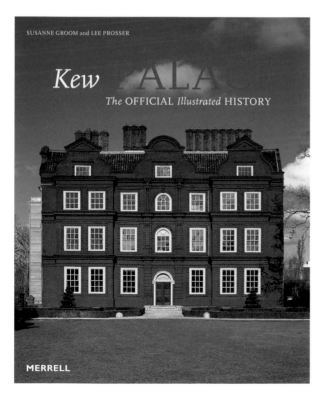

Available from:
The Kew Palace Welcome Centre and all good bookshops

Mail order: mailorder@hrp.org.uk
Tel: +44 (0)870 757 7477
Online: www.historicroyalpalaces.com

In the same series as the Official Illustrated Histories of Hampton Court Palace, Kensington Palace and the Tower of London – available individually or as a boxed set.

Visit our online store for beautiful gifts inspired by centuries of stories from five amazing palaces: **www.historicroyalpalaces.com**

'The Royal family are here always in so very retired a way, that they live as the simplest country gentlefolks.'

(Fanny Burney, Assistant Mistress of the Robes to Queen Charlotte, describing life at Kew in 1786)

Acknowledgements

The Kew Palace project has been supported by the Heritage Lottery Fund with contributions from many individuals, trusts and foundations.

Unless otherwise indicated, the collection on display at Kew Palace belongs to Her Majesty The Queen.

Illustrations

Unless otherwise indicated, all illustrations are © Historic Royal Palaces.

Abbreviations: b = bottom, c = centre, l = left, r = right, t = top

The Bridgeman Art Library, London: pages 6 (Cliveden House, Buckinghamshire), 9tr (© Yale Center for British Art, Paul Mellon Collection, USA); © Copyright The Trustees of The British Museum: pages 14t (BMC 8117), 18-19 (BMC 10368A), 48 (1: BMC 9014), (2: BMC 8080), (3: BMC 7917), 49 (4: BMC 8346), (5: BMC 8616), (6: BMC 8112); © Historic Royal Palaces/newsteam.co.uk. Photograph Nigel Iskander: pages 50c, 51tr; The Madness of King George: pages 42, 43; National Portrait Gallery, London: page 29l; Private Collection, United Kingdom: page 8t; Richmond Local Studies Collection: page 10; Reproduced with the kind permission of the Director and the Board of Trustees, Royal Botanic Gardens, Kew: inside back cover (4, 6, 7, 9, 11-13); The Royal Collection © 2006 Her Majesty Queen Elizabeth II: pages 5, 7, 8bl, 8br, 9tl, 13t, 15b, 24t, 25b, 27r, 28, 34t, 35t; © HM Queen Elizabeth II 2001: page 52tl; The Trustees of the Sir John Soane's Museum: pages 40, 41; Photography by Harland Walshaw harlandwalshaw@hotmail.com: inside back cover (18).

Published by Historic Royal Palaces
Hampton Court Palace
Surrey
KT8 9AU

© Historic Royal Palaces, 2006

ISBN 1 873993 70 6

Written by Sebastian Edwards, unless otherwise indicated
Edited by Sarah Kilby and Clare Murphy
Designed by www.brandremedy.com
Principal photography by Nick Guttridge
Illustrations inside back cover by Robin Wyatt
Printed by Quadracolor

Historic Royal Palaces is a registered charity (no. 1068852).

www.hrp.org.uk

Historic Royal PALACES

Historic Royal Palaces is the independent charity that looks after the Tower of London, Hampton Court Palace, the Banqueting House, Kensington Palace and Kew Palace. We help everyone explore the story of how monarchs and people have shaped society, in some of the greatest palaces ever built.

We receive no funding from the Government or the Crown, so we depend on the support of our visitors, members, donors, volunteers and sponsors.